Published by Gluten-Free by Jan LLC

Gluten-Free by Jan LLC
16067 NW Rondos Dr.
Portland, OR USA 97229-9239

ISBN: 979-8-218-90475-3

Hello, Tagalog!

A First Words Adventure for All Ages

Jeanette Withington
and
Edith Withington

Welcome!

Hello, hello! Kumusta to you!
Let's learn Tagalog words just a few.
Come along, don't be shy,
Our word adventure starts nearby!

araw
(ah-raw)

(ah-raw)

The Sun (Araw)

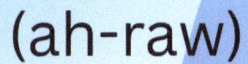

Up in the sky, what do we see?
The Araw shining bright on you
and me.
Golden rays that warm the day,
"Good morning, Araw!" we all
say.

bituin – star
(bee-too-in)

ulap
(oo-lap)

The Cloud (Ulap)
(oo-lap)

A fluffy Ulap drifts so slow.
Soft and white like tip-toe
snow.
Floating gently, passing
through.
"Hello, Ulap! Nice to meet
you!"

ulap
(oo-lap)

mga ibon – birds
(muh-nga ee-bon)

(ee-bon)

The Bird (Ibon)

A chirping Ibon sings a tune,
Dancing lightly, swooping
soon.
With a tweet and tiny hop,
"Ibon's song will never
stop!"

mga puno – trees
(muh-nga poo-no)

The Tree (Puno)

(poo-no)

A tall Puno sways with grace.
Leaves that tickle your smiling face.
Standing strong through every breeze.
"Thank you, Puno, for the shade and trees!"

mga dahon – leaves
(muh-nga dah-hon)

mga bulaklak
(muh-nga boo-lak-lak)

The Flower (Bulaklak)

A bright Bulaklak blooms so sweet.
Petals soft beneath our feet.
Colors glowing in the sun.
"Bulaklak, you're number one!"

bulaklak
(boo-lak-lak)

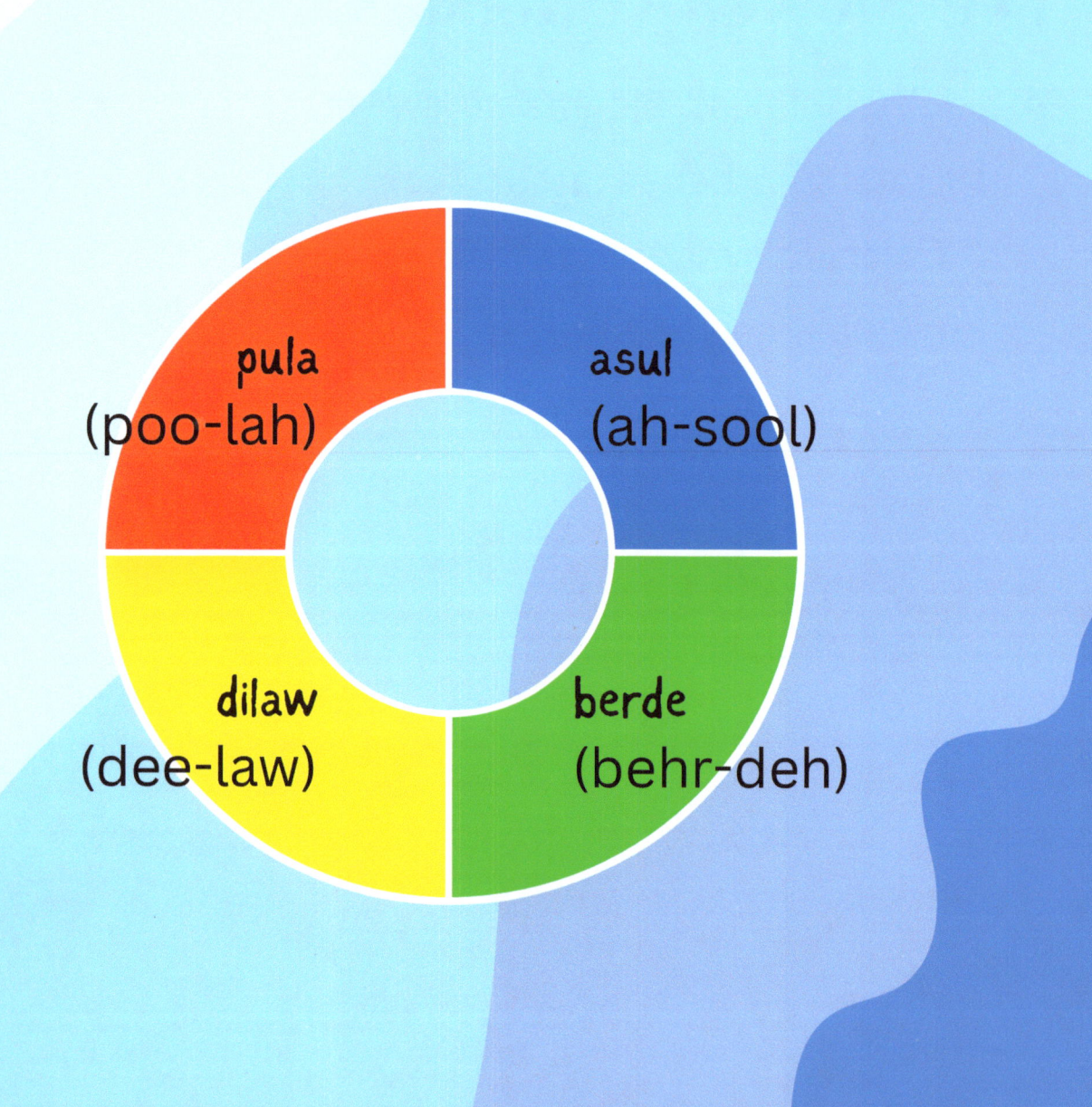

(muh-nga koo-lie)

Colors (Mga Kulay)

Pula for apples, bright and red.

Asul for skies up overhead.

Dilaw for sunshine warm and
light.

Berde for leaves so fresh and
bright.

Colors everywhere you go.

Point and say them nice and
slow!

paruparo – butterfly
(pa-roo-pah-ro)

(muh-nga hah-yop)
Animals (Mga Hayop)

An Aso barks, "Arf! Arf!" loud.

A Pusa purrs, calm and proud.

An Isda swims just watch it flash!

A Paruparo makes wings that splash.

Animal friends from near to far.

Say their names just as they are!

aso
(ah-so)

pusa (poo-sah)

isda
(ees-dah)

kanin
(kah-nin)

saging – banana
(sah-ging)

(pag-ka-een)
Food (Pagkain)

Kanin warm and fluffy white.
Saging sweet. a yummy bite.
Tubig cool and fresh to drink.
You'll say "Ahhh!" before you think.
Snack time's fun for everyone.
Let's eat well before we're done!

kanin – rice
(kah-nin)

tubig – water
(too-big)

it's okay to feel

your feelings

Feelings (Damdamin)

(dam-da-min)

Masaya, happy as can be!
Malungkot, sad oh me, oh my.
Antok, sleepy, rubbing eyes,
maybe time for lullabies.
How you feel is always true.
Share your heart: it's good for you.

masaya
(ma-sah-ya)

malungkot
(ma-long-kot)

antok
(an-took)

nanay – mother
(nah-nye)

tatay – father (tah-tie)

ate – older sister
(ah-teh)

kuya – older brother
(koo-yah)

People We Love

Nanay, a mother, hugs so
warm and tight.
Tatay, a father, smiles with
pure delight.
A Kaibigan, a friend so dear.
With them close, we have no
fear.
Love and laughter every day.
Tagalog words help us say,
"Hooray!"

puso – heart
(poo-so)

kaibigan – friend
(ka-ee-bee-gan)

(pa-ah-lahm)
Goodbye (Paalam)

We learned so much along the
way.
New Tagalog words to speak
and say.
Now it's time to wave goodbye.
Paalam! whispered with a sigh.
But don't you worry, don't you
fear...
Another adventure waits right
here!

www.ingramcontent.com/pod-product-compliance
Lightning Source LLC
Chambersburg PA
CBHW041607120626

46551CB00002B/348